LOOK, STRA

Look, Stranger!

W. H. AUDEN

ff

faber and faber

First published in 1936
by Faber and Faber Limited
3 Queen Square London WC1N 3AU
This paperback edition first published in 2001

Photoset by Wilmaset Ltd, Wirral
Printed in England by MPG Books Limited,
Victoria Square, Bodmin, Cornwall

A CIP record for this book
is available from the British Library
ISBN 0-571-20764-2

2 4 6 8 10 9 7 5 3 1

TO ERIKA MANN

Since the external disorder, and extravagant lies,
The baroque frontiers, the surrealist police;
What can truth treasure, or heart bless,
But a narrow strictness?

Contents

1 Prologue

O love, the interest itself in thoughtless Heaven
Make simpler daily the beating of man's heart; within,
There in the ring where name and image meet,

Inspire them with such a longing as will make his thought
Alive like patterns a murmuration of starlings
Rising in joy over wolds unwittingly weave;

Here too on our little reef display your power,
This fortress perched on the edge of the Atlantic scarp,
The mole between all Europe and the exile-crowded sea;

And make us as Newton was, who in his garden watching
The apple falling towards England, became aware
Between himself and her of an eternal tie.

For now that dream which so long has contented our will,
I mean, of uniting the dead into a splendid empire,
Under whose fertilising flood the Lancashire moss

Sprouted up chimneys, and Glamorgan hid a life
Grim as a tidal rock-pool's in its glove-shaped valleys,
Is already retreating into her maternal shadow;

Leaving the furnaces gasping in the impossible air,
The flotsam at which Dumbarton gapes and hungers;
While upon wind-loved Rowley no hammer shakes

The cluster of mounds like a midget golf course, graves
Of some who created these intelligible dangerous marvels;
Affectionate people, but crude their sense of glory.

Far-sighted as falcons, they looked down another future;
For the seed in their loins were hostile, though afraid of their
    pride,
And, tall with a shadow now, inertly wait.

In bar, in netted chicken-farm, in lighthouse,
Standing on these impoverished constricting acres,
The ladies and gentlemen apart, too much alone,

Consider the years of the measured world begun,
The barren spiritual marriage of stone and water.
Yet, O, at this very moment of our hopeless sigh

When inland they are thinking their thoughts but are
    watching these islands,
As children in Chester look to Moel Fammau to decide
On picnics by the clearness or withdrawal of her treeless
    crown,

Some possible dream, long coiled in the ammonite's slumber
Is uncurling, prepared to lay on our talk and kindness
Its military silence, its surgeon's idea of pain;

And out of the Future into actual History,
As when Merlin, tamer of horses, and his lords to whom
Stonehenge was still a thought, the Pillars passed

And into the undared ocean swung north their prow,
Drives through the night and star-concealing dawn
For the virgin roadsteads of our hearts an unwavering keel.

II

(*To Geoffrey Hoyland*)

Out on the lawn I lie in bed,
Vega conspicuous overhead
    In the windless nights of June;
Forests of green have done complete
The day's activity; my feet
    Point to the rising moon.

Lucky, this point in time and space
Is chosen as my working place;
    Where the sexy airs of summer,
The bathing hours and the bare arms,
The leisured drives through a land of farms,
    Are good to the newcomer.

Equal with colleagues in a ring
I sit on each calm evening,
    Enchanted as the flowers
The opening light draws out of hiding
From leaves with all its dove-like pleading
    Its logic and its powers.

That later we, though parted then
May still recall these evenings when
    Fear gave his watch no look;
The lion griefs loped from the shade
And on our knees their muzzles laid,
    And Death put down his book.

[3]

Moreover, eyes in which I learn
That I am glad to look, return
    My glances every day;
And when the birds and rising sun
Waken me, I shall speak with one
    Who has not gone away.

Now North and South and East and West
Those I love lie down to rest;
    The moon looks on them all:
The healers and the brilliant talkers,
The eccentrics and the silent walkers,
    The dumpy and the tall.

She climbs the European sky;
Churches and power stations lie
    Alike among earth's fixtures:
Into the galleries she peers,
And blankly as an orphan stares
    Upon the marvellous pictures.

To gravity attentive, she
Can notice nothing here; though we
    Whom hunger cannot move,
From gardens where we feel secure
Look up, and with a sigh endure
    The tyrannies of love:

And, gentle, do not care to know,
Where Poland draws her Eastern bow,
    What violence is done;
Nor ask what doubtful act allows
Our freedom in this English house,
    Our picnics in the sun.

The creepered wall stands up to hide
The gathering multitudes outside
    Whose glances hunger worsens;
Concealing from their wretchedness
Our metaphysical distress,
    Our kindness to ten persons.

And now no path on which we move
But shows already traces of
    Intentions not our own,
Thoroughly able to achieve
What our excitement could conceive,
    But our hands left alone.

For what by nature and by training
We loved, has little strength remaining:
    Though we would gladly give
The Oxford colleges, Big Ben,
And all the birds in Wicken Fen,
    It has no wish to live.

Soon through the dykes of our content
The crumpling flood will force a rent,
    And, taller than a tree,
Hold sudden death before our eyes
Whose river-dreams long hid the size
    And vigours of the sea.

But when the waters make retreat
And through the black mud first the wheat
    In shy green stalks appears;
When stranded monsters gasping lie,
And sounds of riveting terrify
    Their whorled unsubtle ears:

May this for which we dread to lose
Our privacy, need no excuse
    But to that strength belong;
As through a child's rash happy cries
The drowned voice of his parents rise
    In unlamenting song.

After discharges of alarm,
All unpredicted may it calm
    The pulse of nervous nations;
Forgive the murderer in his glass,
Tough in its patience to surpass
    The tigress her swift motions.

III

Our hunting fathers told the story
   Of the sadness of the creatures,
Pitied the limits and the lack
   Set in their finished features;
Saw in the lion's intolerant look,
Behind the quarry's dying glare,
Love raging for the personal glory
   That reason's gift would add,
The liberal appetite and power,
   The rightness of a god.

Who nurtured in that fine tradition
   Predicted the result,
Guessed love by nature suited to
   The intricate ways of guilt?
That human ligaments could so
His southern gestures modify,
And make it his mature ambition
   To think no thought but ours,
To hunger, work illegally,
   And be anonymous?

IV Song

Let the florid music praise,
    The flute and the trumpet,
Beauty's conquest of your face:
In that land of flesh and bone,
Where from citadels on high
Her imperial standards fly,
    Let the hot sun
    Shine on, shine on.

O but the unloved have had power,
    The weeping and striking,
Always; time will bring their hour:
Their secretive children walk
Through your vigilance of breath
To unpardonable death,
    And my vows break
    Before his look.

V

Look, stranger, at this island now
The leaping light for your delight discovers,
Stand stable here
And silent be,
That through the channels of the ear
May wander like a river
The swaying sound of the sea.

Here at the small field's ending pause
Where the chalk wall falls to the foam, and its tall ledges
Oppose the pluck
And knock of the tide,
And the shingle scrambles after the suck-
-ing surf, and the gull lodges
A moment on its sheer side.

Far off like floating seeds the ships
Diverge on urgent voluntary errands;
And the full view
Indeed may enter
And move in memory as now these clouds do,
That pass the harbour mirror
And all the summer through the water saunter.

O what is that sound which so thrills the ear
   Down in the valley drumming, drumming?
Only the scarlet soldiers, dear,
      The soldiers coming.

O what is that light I see flashing so clear
   Over the distance brightly, brightly?
Only the sun on their weapons, dear,
      As they step lightly.

O what are they doing with all that gear;
   What are they doing this morning, this morning?
Only the usual manœuvres, dear,
      Or perhaps a warning.

O why have they left the road down there;
   Why are they suddenly wheeling, wheeling?
Perhaps a change in the orders, dear;
      Why are you kneeling?

O haven't they stopped for the doctor's care;
   Haven't they reined their horses, their horses?
Why, they are none of them wounded, dear,
      None of these forces.

O is it the parson they want with white hair;
   Is it the parson, is it, is it?
No, they are passing his gateway, dear,
      Without a visit.

O it must be the farmer who lives so near;
   It must be the farmer so cunning, so cunning?

They have passed the farm already, dear,
    And now they are running.

O where are they going? stay with me here!
  Were the vows you swore me deceiving, deceiving?
No, I promised to love you, dear,
    But I must be leaving.

O it's broken the lock and splintered the door,
  O it's the gate where they're turning, turning;
Their feet are heavy on the floor
    And their eyes are burning.

Hearing of harvests rotting in the valleys,
Seeing at end of street the barren mountains,
Round corners coming suddenly on water,
Knowing them shipwrecked who were launched for islands,
We honour founders of these starving cities,
Whose honour is the image of our sorrow.

Which cannot see its likeness in their sorrow
That brought them desperate to the brink of valleys;
Dreaming of evening walks through learned cities,
They reined their violent horses on the mountains,
Those fields like ships to castaways on islands, ·
Visions of green to them that craved for water.

They built by rivers and at night the water
Running past windows comforted their sorrow;
Each in his little bed conceived of islands
Where every day was dancing in the valleys,
And all the year trees blossomed on the mountains,
Where love was innocent, being far from cities.

But dawn came back and they were still in cities;
No marvellous creature rose up from the water,
There was still gold and silver in the mountains,
And hunger was a more immediate sorrow;
Although to moping villagers in valleys
Some waving pilgrims were describing islands.

'The gods', they promised, 'visit us from islands,
Are stalking head-up, lovely through the cities;
Now is the time to leave your wretched valleys
And sail with them across the lime-green water;

Sitting at their white sides, forget their sorrow,
The shadow cast across your lives by mountains.'

So many, doubtful, perished in the mountains
Climbing up crags to get a view of islands;
So many, fearful, took with them their sorrow
Which stayed them when they reached unhappy cities;
So many, careless, dived and drowned in water;
So many, wretched, would not leave their valleys.

It is the sorrow; shall it melt? Ah, water
Would gush, flush, green these mountains and these valleys,
And we rebuild our cities, not dream of islands.

VIII

Now the leaves are falling fast,
Nurse's flowers will not last;
Nurses to the graves are gone,
And the prams go rolling on.

Whispering neighbours, left and right,
Pluck us from the real delight;
And the active hands must freeze
Lonely on the separate knees.

Dead in hundreds at the back
Follow wooden in our track,
Arms raised stiffly to reprove
In false attitudes of love.

Starving through the leafless wood
Trolls run scolding for their food;
And the nightingale is dumb,
And the angel will not come.

Cold, impossible, ahead
Lifts the mountain's lovely head
Whose white waterfall could bless
Travellers in their last distress.

IX

The earth turns over, our side feels the cold,
And life sinks choking in the wells of trees;
The ticking heart comes to a standstill, killed,
The icing on the pond waits for the boys.
Among the holly and the gifts I move,
The carols on the piano, the glowing hearth,
All our traditional sympathy with birth,
Put by your challenge to the shifts of love.

Your portrait hangs before me on the wall
And there what wish I wish for, I shall find,
The wooded or the stony – though not all
The painter's gifts can make its flatness round –
Through the blue irises the heaven of failures,
The mirror world where logic is reversed,
Where age becomes the handsome child at last,
The glass sea parted for the country sailors.

Where move the enormous comics, drawn from life;
My father as an Airedale and a gardener,
My mother chasing letters with a knife:
You are not present as a character.
– Only the family have speaking parts –
You are a valley or a river bend,
The one an aunt refers to as a friend,
The tree from which the weasel racing starts.

False; but no falser than the world it matches,
Love's daytime kingdom which I say you rule,
The total state where all must wear your badges,
Keep order perfect as a naval school:

Noble emotions organized and massed
Line the straight flood-lit tracks of memory
To cheer your image as it flashes by;
All lust at once informed on and suppressed.

Yours is the only name expressive there,
And family affection the one in cypher;
Lay-out of hospital and street and square
That comfort to the homesick children offer:
As I, their author, stand between these dreams,
Son of a nurse and doctor, loaned a dream,
Your would-be lover who has never come
In the great bed at midnight to your arms.

Such dreams are amorous; they are indeed:
But no one but myself is loved in these,
And time flies on above the dreamer's head,
Flies on, flies on, and with your beauty flies.
All things he takes and loses but conceit,
The Alec who can buy the life within,
License no liberty except his own,
Order the fireworks after the defeat.

Language of moderation cannot hide;
My sea is empty and the waves are rough:
Gone from the map the shore where childhood played
Tight-fisted as a peasant, eating love;
Lost in my wake the archipelago,
Islands of self through which I sailed all day,
Planting a pirate's flag, a generous boy;
And lost the way to action and to you.

Lost if I steer. Gale of desire may blow
Sailor and ship past the illusive reef,
And I yet land to celebrate with you

Birth of a natural order and of love;
With you enjoy the untransfigured scene,
My father down the garden in his gaiters,
My mother at her bureau writing letters,
Free to our favours, all our titles gone.

X

Now from my window-sill I watch the night
The church clock's yellow face, the green pier light
Burn for a new imprudent year;
The silence buzzes in my ear;
The jets in both the dormitories are out.

Under the darkness nothing seems to stir;
The lilac bush like a conspirator
Shams dead upon the lawn and there
Above the flagstaff the Great Bear
Hangs as a portent over Helensburgh.

But deaf to prophecy or China's drum
The blood moves strangely in its moving home,
Diverges, loops to travel further
Than the long still shadow of the father,
Though to the valley of regret it come.

Now in this season when the ice is loosened,
In scrubbed laboratories research is hastened
And cameras at the growing wood
Are pointed; for the long lost good,
Desire like a police-dog is unfastened.

O Lords of limit, training dark and light
And setting a tabu 'twixt left and right:
The influential quiet twins
From whom all property begins,
Look leniently upon us all to-night.

Oldest of masters, whom the schoolboy fears
Failing to find his pen, to keep back tears,

Collecting stamps and butterflies
Hoping in some way to appease
The malice of the erratic examiners.

No one has seen you. None can say of late,
'Here – you can see the marks – they lay in wait.'
But in my thought to-night you seem
Forms which I saw once in a dream,
The stocky keepers of a wild estate.

With guns beneath your arms, in sun and wet
At doorways posted or on ridges set,
By copse or bridge we know you there
Whose sleepless presences endear
Our peace to us with a perpetual threat.

We know you moody, silent, sensitive,
Quick to be offended, slow to forgive,
But to your discipline the heart
Submits when we have fallen apart
Into the isolated personal life.

Look not too closely, but not over-quick;
We have no invitation, but we are sick,
Using the mole's device, the carriage
Of peacock or rat's desperate courage,
For we shall only pass you by a trick.

At the end of my corridor are boys who dream
Of a new bicycle or winning team;
On their behalf guard all the more
This late-maturing Northern shore,
Who to their serious season must shortly come.

Give them spontaneous skill at holding rein,
At twisting dial, or at making fun,

That these may never need our craft,
Who, awkward, pasty, feeling the draught,
Have health and skill and beauty on the brain.

The clocks strike ten: the tea is on the stove;
And up the stair come voices that I love.
Love, satisfaction, force, delight,
To these players of Badminton to-night,
To Favel, Holland, sprightly Alexis give.

Deeper towards the summer the year moves on.
And what if the starving visionary have seen
The carnival within our gates,
Your bodies kicked about the streets,
We need your power still: use it, that none

O from this table break uncontrollably away
Lunging, insensible to injury,
Dangerous in the room, or out wild-
-ly spinning like a top in the field,
Mopping and mowing through the sleepless day.

Just as his dream foretold, he met them all:
The smiling grimy boy at the garage
Ran out before he blew his horn; the tall
Professor in the mountains with his large
Tweed pockets full of plants addressed him hours
Before he would have dared: the deaf girl too
Seemed to expect him at the green chateau;
The meal was laid, the guest room full of flowers.

More, the talk always took the wished-for turn,
Dwelt on the need for stroking and advice;
Yet, at each meeting, he was forced to learn,
The same misunderstanding would arise.
Which was in need of help? Were they or he
The physician, bridegroom and incendiary?

As it is, plenty;
As it's admitted
The children happy
And the car, the car
That goes so far
And the wife devoted:
To this as it is,
To the work and the banks
Let his thinning hair
And his hauteur
Give thanks, give thanks.

All that was thought
As like as not, is not;
When nothing was enough
But love, but love
And the rough future
Of an intransigent nature
And the betraying smile,
Betraying, but a smile:
That that is not, is not;
Forget, Forget.

Let him not cease to praise
Then his spacious days;
Yes, and the success
Let him bless, let him bless:
Let him see in this
The profits larger
And the sins venal,

Lest he see as it is
The loss as major
And final, final.

XIII

A shilling life will give you all the facts:
How Father beat him, how he ran away,
What were the struggles of his youth, what acts
Made him the greatest figure of his day:
Of how he fought, fished, hunted, worked all night,
Though giddy, climbed new mountains; named a sea:
Some of the last researchers even write
Love made him weep his pints like you and me.

With all his honours on, he sighed for one
Who, say astonished critics, lived at home;
Did little jobs about the house with skill
And nothing else; could whistle; would sit still
Or potter round the garden; answered some
Of his long marvellous letters but kept none.

Brothers, who when the sirens roar
From office, shop and factory pour
      'Neath evening sky;
By cops directed to the fug
Of talkie-houses for a drug,
Or down canals to find a hug
      Until you die:

We know, remember, what it is
That keeps you celebrating this
      Sad ceremonial;
We know the terrifying brink
From which in dreams you nightly shrink
'I shall be sacked without', you think,
      'A testimonial.'

We cannot put on airs with you
The fears that hurt you hurt us too
      Only we say
That like all nightmares these are fake
If you would help us we could make
Our eyes to open, and awake
      Shall find night day.

On you our interests are set
Your sorrow we shall not forget
      While we consider
Those who in every county town
For centuries have done you down,
But you shall see them tumble down
      Both horse and rider.

O splendid person, you who stand
In spotless flannels or with hand
        Expert on trigger;
Whose lovely hair and shapely limb
Year after year are kept in trim
Till buffers envy as you swim
        Your Grecian figure:

You are not jealous yet, we know,
But we must warn you, even so
        So pray be seated:
It isn't cricket, but it's true
The lady who admires us, you
Have thought you're getting off with too,
        For you're conceited.

Your beauty's a completed thing.
The future kissed you, called you king,
        Did she? Deceiver!
She's not in love with you at all
No feat of yours can make her fall,
She will not answer to your call
        Like your retriever.

Dare-devil mystic who bears the scars
Of many spiritual wars
        And smoothly tell
The starving that their one starvation
Is personal regeneration
By fasting, prayer and contemplation;
        Is it? Well,

Others have tried it, all delight
Sustained in that ecstatic flight
        Could not console

When through exhausting hours they'd flown
From the alone to the Alone,
Nothing remained but the dry-as-bone
        Night of the soul.

Coward; for all your goodness game
Your dream of Heaven is the same
        As any bounder's;
You hope to corner as reward
All that the rich can here afford
Love and music and bed and board
        While the world flounders.

And you, the wise man, full of humour
To whom our misery's a rumour
        And slightly funny;
Proud of your nicely balanced view
You say as if it were something new
The fuss we make is mostly due
        To lack of money.

Ah, what a little squirt is there
When of your aren't-I-charming air
        You stand denuded.
Behind your subtle sense of humour
You hide the boss's simple stuma,
Among the foes which we enumer
        You are included.

Because you saw but were not indignant
The invasion of the great malignant
        Cambridge ulcer
That army intellectual
Of every kind of liberal

Smarmy with friendship but of all
    There are none falser.

A host of columbines and pathics
Who show the poor by mathematics
    In their defence
That wealth and poverty are merely
Mental pictures, so that clearly
Every tramp's a landlord really
  In mind-events.

Let fever sweat them till they tremble
Cramp rack their limbs till they resemble
    Cartoons by Goya:
Their daughters sterile be in rut,
May cancer rot their herring gut,
The circular madness on them shut,
    Or paranoia.

Their splendid people, their wiseacres,
Professors, agents, magic-makers,
    Their poets and apostles,
Their bankers and their brokers too,
And ironmasters shall turn blue
Shall fade away like morning dew
    With club-room fossils.

The chimneys are smoking, the crocus is out in the border;
The mountain ranges are massive in the blue March day;
Like a sea god the political orator lands at the pier;

> But, O, my magnet, my pomp, my beauty
> More telling to heart than the sea,
> Than Europe or my own home town
> To-day is parted from me
> And I stand on our world alone.

Over the town now, in for an hour from the desert
A hawk looks down on us all; he is not in this;
Our kindness is hid from the eye of the vivid creature;

> Sees only the configuration of field,
> Copse, chalk-pit, and fallow,
> The distribution of forces,
> The play of sun and shadow
> On upturned faces.

For the game is in progress which tends to become like a war,
The contest of the Whites with the Reds for the carried thing
Divided in secret among us, a portion to each:

> That power which gave us our lives
> Gave us, we found when we met,
> Out of the complex to be reassembled
> Pieces that fit,
> Whereat with love we trembled.

Last week we embraced on the dunes and thought they were
    pleased;
Now lake and holes in the mountains remind us of error,
Strolling in the valley we are uncertain of the trees:

Their shadow falls upon us;
Are they spies on the human heart
Motionless, tense in the hope
Of catching us out? Are they hostile, apart
From the belovèd group?

For our hour of unity makes us aware of two worlds;
That was revealed to us then in our double-shadow,
Which for the masters of harbours, the colliers, and us,
For our calculating star,
Where the divided feel
Tears in their eyes
And time and doctors heal,
Eternally sighs.

Yes, the white death, friendless, has his own idea of us;
We're something far more exciting than just friends.
He has his private saga he tells himself at night,
Which starts with the handsome couple
Estranged by a mistake,
Follows their lifetime curses,
Ends with the fruitless rescue from the lake,
Their death-bed kisses.

Then lightly, my darling, leave me and slip away
Playful, betraying him nothing, allaying suspicion:
His eye is on all these people about us, leading
Their quiet horrified lives,
But if we can trust we are free,
Though alone among those
Who within earshot of the ungovernable sea
Grow set in their ways.

We ride a turning globe, we stand on a star;
It has thrust us up together; it is stronger than we.

In it our separate sorrows are a single hope,
    It's in its nature always to appear
    Behind us as we move
    With linked arms through our dreams,
    Wherefore, apart, we love
    Its sundering streams.

And since our desire cannot take that route which is
    straightest,
Let us choose the crooked, so implicating these acres,
These millions in whom already the wish to be one
    Like a burglar is stealthily moving,
    That these, on the new façade of a bank
    Employed, or conferring at health resort,
    May, by circumstance linked,
    More clearly act our thought.

Then dance, the boatmen, virgins, camera-men and us
Round goal-post, wind-gauge, pylon or bobbing buoy;
For our joy abounding is, though it hide underground,
    As insect or camouflaged cruiser
    For fear of death sham dead,
    Is quick, is real, is quick to answer
    The bird-like sucking tread
    Of the quick dancer.

XVI

May with its light behaving
Stirs vessel, eye, and limb;
The singular and sad
Are willing to recover,
And to the swan-delighting river
The careless picnics come,
The living white and red.

The dead remote and hooded
In their enclosures rest; but we
From the vague woods have broken,
Forests where children meet
And the white angel-vampires flit;
We stand with shaded eye,
The dangerous apple taken.

The real world lies before us;
Animal motions of the young,
The common wish for death,
The pleasured and the haunted;
The dying master sinks tormented
In the admirers' ring,
The unjust walk the earth.

And love that makes impatient
The tortoise and the roe, and lays
The blonde beside the dark,
Urges upon our blood,
Before the evil and the good
How insufficient is
The endearment and the look.

Here on the cropped grass of the narrow ridge I stand,
A fathom of earth, alive in air,
Aloof as an admiral on the old rocks,
   England below me:
Eastward across the Midland plains
An express is leaving for a sailor's country;
   Westward is Wales
Where on clear evenings the retired and rich
From the french windows of their sheltered mansions
See the Sugarloaf standing, an upright sentinel
   Over Abergavenny.

When last I stood here I was not alone; happy
Each thought the other, thinking of a crime,
And England to our meditations seemed
   The perfect setting:
But now it has no innocence at all;
It is the isolation and the fear,
   The mood itself;
It is the body of the absent lover,
An image to the would-be hero of the soul,
The little area we are willing to forgive
   Upon conditions.

For private reasons I must have the truth, remember
These years have seen a boom in sorrow;
The presses of idleness issued more despair
   And it was honoured,
Gross Hunger took on more hands every month,
Erecting here and everywhere his vast
   Unnecessary workshops;

[33]

Europe grew anxious about her health,
Combines tottered, credits froze,
And business shivered in a banker's winter
    While we were kissing.

To-day no longer occupied like that, I give
The children at the open swimming pool
Lithe in their first and little beauty
    A closer look;
Follow the cramped clerk crooked at his desk,
The guide in shorts pursuing flowers
    In their careers;
A digit of the crowd, would like to know
Them better whom the shops and trams are full of,
The little men and their mothers, not plain but
    Dreadfully ugly.

Deaf to the Welsh wind now, I hear arising
From lanterned gardens sloping to the river
Where saxophones are moaning for a comforter,
    From Gaumont theatres
Where fancy plays on hunger to produce
The noble robber, ideal of boys,
    And from cathedrals,
Luxury liners laden with souls,
Holding to the east their hulls of stone,
The high thin rare continuous worship
    Of the self-absorbed.

Here, which looked north before the Cambrian alignment,
Like the cupped hand of the keen excavator
Busy with bones, the memory uncovers
    The hopes of time;

Of empires stiff in their brocaded glory,
The luscious lateral blossoming of woe
    Scented, profuse;
And of intercalary ages of disorder
When, as they prayed in antres, fell
Upon the noblest in the country night
    Angel assassins.

Small birds above me have the grace of those who founded
The civilization of the delicate olive,
Learning the laws of love and sailing
    On the calm Aegean;
The hawk is the symbol of the rule by thirst,
The central state controlling the canals;
    And the blank sky
Of the womb's utter peace before
The cell, dividing, multiplied desire,
And raised instead of death the image
    Of the reconciler.

And over the Cotswolds now the thunder mutters:
'What little of the truth your seers saw
They dared not tell you plainly but combined
    Assertion and refuge
In the common language of collective lying,
In codes of a bureau, laboratory slang
    And diplomats' French.
The relations of your lovers were, alas, pictorial;
The treasure that you stole, you lost; bad luck
It brought you, but you cannot put it back
    Now with caresses.

'Already behind you your last evening hastens up
And all the customs your society has chosen

Hardens themselves into the unbreakable
    Habits of death,
Has not your long affair with death
Of late become increasingly more serious;
    Do you not find
Him growing more attractive every day?
You shall go under and help him with the crops,
Be faithful to him, and to your friends
    Remain indifferent.'

And out of the turf the bones of war continue;
'Know then, cousin, the major cause of our collapse
Was a distortion in the human plastic by luxury produced,

Never higher than in our time were the vital advantages;
To matter entire, to the unbounded vigours of the instrument,
To all logical precision we were the rejoicing heirs.

But pompous, we assumed their power to be our own,
Believed machines to be our hearts' spontaneous fruit,
Taking our premises as shoppers take a tram.

While the disciplined love which alone could have employed
    these engines
Seemed far too difficult and dull, and when hatred promised
An immediate dividend, all of us hated.

Denying the liberty we knew quite well to be our destiny,
It dogged our steps with its accusing shadow
Until in every landscape we saw murder ambushed.

Unable to endure ourselves, we sought relief
In the insouciance of the soldier, the heroic sexual pose
Playing at fathers to impress the little ladies,

[36]

Call us not tragic; falseness made farcical our death:
Nor brave; ours was the will of the insane to suffer
By which since we could not live we gladly died:
And now we have gone for ever to our foolish graves.'

The Priory clock chimes briefly and I recollect
I am expected to return alive
My will effective and my nerves in order
   To my situation.
'The poetry is in the pity,' Wilfred said,
And Kathy in her journal, 'To be rooted in life,
   That's what I want.'
These moods give no permission to be idle,
For men are changed by what they do;
And through loss and anger the hands of the unlucky
   Love one another.

The sun shines down on the ships at sea,
It shines on you and it shines on me
Whatever we are or are going to be.

Tomorrow if everything goes to plan,
Tomorrow morning you'll be a man:
Let wishes be horses as fast as they can.

    The dogs are barking, the crops are growing,
    But nobody knows how the wind is blowing:
    Gosh, to look at we're no great catch;
    History seems to have struck a bad patch.

    We haven't the time – it's been such a rush –
    Except to attend to our own little push:
    The teacher setting examinations,
    The journalist writing his falsifications,

    The poet reciting to Lady Diana
    While the footmen whisper 'Have a banana',
    The judge enforcing the obsolete law,
    The banker making the loan for the war,

    The expert designing the long-range gun
    To exterminate everyone under the sun,
    Would like to get out but could only mutter; –
    'What can I do? It's my bread and butter.'

In your house tonight you are flushed and gay;
Twenty-one years have passed away;
Tomorrow morning's another day.

To lie flat on the back with the knees flexed
And sunshine on the soft receptive belly,
Or face down, the insolent spine relaxed,
No more compelled to cower or to bully,
Is good; and good to see them passing by
Below on the white sidewalk in the heat,
The dog, the lady with parcels, and the boy:
There is the casual life outside the heart.

Yes, we are out of sight and earshot here.
Are you aware what weapon you are loading,
To what that teasing talk is quietly leading?
Our pulses count but do not judge the hour.
Who are you with, from whom you turn away,
At whom you dare not look? Do you know why?

XX

Fleeing the short-haired mad executives,
The subtle useless faces round my home,
Upon the mountains of our fear I climb;
Above, the breakneck scorching rock, the caves;
No col, no water; with excuse concocted,
Soon on a lower alp I fall and pant,
Cooling my face there in the faults that flaunt
The life which they have stolen and perfected.

Climbing with you was easy as a vow;
We reached the top not hungry in the least;
But it was eyes we looked at, not the view;
Saw nothing but ourselves, left-handed, lost:
Returned to shore, the rich interior still
Unknown. Love gave the power, but took the will.

Easily, my dear, you move, easily your head
And easily as through the leaves of a photograph album I'm led
Through the night's delights and the day's impressions,
Past the tall tenements and the trees in the wood;
Though sombre the sixteen skies of Europe
  And the Danube flood.

Looking and loving our behaviours pass
The stones the steels and the polished glass;
Lucky to Love the new pansy railway,
The sterile farms where his looks are fed,
And in the policed unlucky city
  Lucky his bed.

He from these lands of terrifying mottoes
Makes worlds as innocent as Beatrix Potter's;
Through bankrupt countries where they mend the roads
Along the endless plains his will is
Intent as a collector to pursue
  His greens and lilies.

Easy for him to find in your face
The pool of silence and the tower of grace,
To conjure a camera into a wishing rose;
Simple to excite in the air from a glance
The horses, the fountains, the sidedrum, the trombone
  And the dance, the dance.

Summoned by such a music from our time,
Such images to audience come
As vanity cannot dispel nor bless:
Hunger and love in their variations

Grouped invalids watching the flight of the birds
        And single assassins.

Ten thousand of the desperate marching by
Five feet, six feet, seven feet high:
Hitler and Mussolini in their wooing poses
Churchill acknowledging the voter's greeting
Roosevelt at the microphone, Van der Lubbe laughing
        And our first meeting.

But love, except at our proposal,
Will do no trick at his disposal;
Without opinions of his own, performs
The programme that we think of merit,
And through our private stuff must work
        His public spirit.

Certain it became while we were still incomplete
There were certain prizes for which we would never compete;
A choice was killed by every childish illness,
The boiling tears among the hothouse plants,
The rigid promise fractured in the garden,
        And the long aunts.

And every day there bolted from the field
Desires to which we could not yield;
Fewer and clearer grew the plans,
Schemes for a life and sketches for a hatred,
And early among my interesting scrawls
        Appeared your portrait.

You stand now before me, flesh and bone
These ghosts would like to make their own.
Are they your choices? O, be deaf
When hatred would proffer her immediate pleasure,

[42]

And glory swap her fascinating rubbish
        For your one treasure.

Be deaf too, standing uncertain now,
A pine tree shadow across your brow,
To what I hear and wish I did not;
The voice of love saying lightly, brightly –
'Be Lubbe, Be Hitler, but be my good
        Daily, nightly'.

The power that corrupts, that power to excess
The beautiful quite naturally possess:
To them the fathers and the children turn:
And all who long for their destruction,
The arrogant and self-insulted, wait
        The looked instruction.

Shall idleness ring then your eyes like the pest?
O will you unnoticed and mildly like the rest,
Will you join the lost in their sneering circles,
Forfeit the beautiful interest and fall
Where the engaging face is the face of the betrayer,
        And the pang is all?

Wind shakes the tree; the mountains darken;
And the heart repeats though we would not hearken:
'Yours is the choice, to whom the gods awarded
The language of learning and the language of love,
Crooked to move as a moneybug or a cancer
        Or straight as a dove.'

XXII Two Songs

(For Benjamin Britten)

I

Night covers up the rigid land
　　And ocean's quaking moor,
And shadows with a tolerant hand
　　The ugly and the poor.

The wounded pride for which I weep
　　You cannot staunch, nor I
Control the moments of your sleep,
　　Nor hear the name you cry,

Whose life is lucky in your eyes,
　　And precious is the bed
As to his utter fancy lies
　　The dark caressive head.

For each love to its aim is true,
　　And all kinds seek their own;
You love your life and I love you,
　　So I must lie alone.

O hurry to the fêted spot
　　Of your deliberate fall;
For now my dream of you cannot
　　Refer to you at all.

Underneath the abject willow,
   Lover, sulk no more;
Act from thought should quickly follow:
   What is thinking for?
Your unique and moping station
   Proved you cold;
   Stand up and fold
Your map of desolation.

Bells that toll across the meadows
   From the sombre spire,
Toll for those unloving shadows
   Love does not require.
All that lives may love; why longer
   Bow to loss
   With arms across?
Strike and you shall conquer.

Geese in flocks above you flying
   Their direction know;
Brooks beneath the thin ice flowing
   To their oceans go;
Coldest love will warm to action,
   Walk then, come,
   No longer numb,
Into your satisfaction.

XXIII

To settle in this village of the heart,
My darling, can you bear it? True, the hall
With its yews and famous dovecots is still there
Just as in childhood, but the grand old couple
Who loved us all so equally are dead;
And now it is a licensed house for tourists,
None too particular. One of the new
Trunk roads passes the very door already,
And the thin cafés spring up over night.
The sham ornamentation, the strident swimming pool,
The identical and townee smartness,
Will you really see as home, and not depend
For comfort on the chance, the sly encounter
With the irresponsible beauty of the stranger?
O can you see precisely in our gauchness
The neighbour's strongest wish, to serve and love?

O for doors to be open and an invite with gilded edges
To dine with Lord Lobcock and Count Asthma on the
    platinum benches,
With the somersaults and fireworks, the roads and the
    smacking kisses –
        Cried the cripples to the silent statue,
        The six beggared cripples.

And Garbo's and Cleopatra's wits to go astraying,
In a feather ocean with me to go fishing and playing
Still jolly when the cock has burst himself with crowing –
        Cried the six cripples to the silent statue,
        The six beggared cripples.

And to stand on green turf among the craning yelling faces,
Dependent on the chestnut, the sable, and Arabian horses,
And me with a magic crystal to foresee their places –
        Cried the six cripples to the silent statue,
        The six beggared cripples.

And this square to be a deck, and these pigeons sail to rig
And to follow the delicious breeze like a tantony pig
To the shaded feverless islands where the melons are big –
        Cried the six cripples to the silent statue,
        The six beggared cripples

And these shops to be turned to tulips in a garden bed,
And me with my stick to thrash each merchant dead
As he pokes from a flower his bald and wicked head –
        Cried the six cripples to the silent statue,
        The six beggared cripples.

And a hole in the bottom of heaven, and Peter and Paul
And each smug surprised saint like parachutes to fall,
And every one-legged beggar to have no legs at all –
      Cried the six cripples to the silent statue,
      The six beggared cripples.

xxv Casino

Only the hands are living; to the wheel attracted,
Are moved, as deer trek desperately towards a creek
Through the dust and scrub of the desert, or gently
   As sunflowers turn to the light.

And as the night takes up the cries of feverish children,
The cravings of lions in dens, the loves of dons,
   Gathers them all and remains the night, the
   Great room is full of their prayers.

To the last feast of isolation, self-invited,
They flock, and in the rite of disbelief are joined;
   From numbers all their stars are recreated,
   The enchanted, the world, the sad.

Without, the rivers flow among the wholly living,
Quite near their trysts; and the mountains part them; and the
     bird,
   Deep in the greens and moistures of summer,
   Sings towards their work.

But here no nymph comes naked to the youngest shepherd,
The fountain is deserted, the laurel will not grow;
   The labyrinth is safe but endless, and broken
   Is Ariadne's thread.

As deeper in these hands is grooved their fortune: 'Lucky
Were few, and it is possible that none were loved;
   And what was godlike in this generation
   Was never to be born.'

XXVI

That night when joy began
Our narrowest veins to flush
We waited for the flash
Of morning's levelled gun.

But morning let us pass
And day by day relief
Outgrew his nervous laugh;
Grows credulous of peace

As mile by mile is seen
No trespasser's reproach
And love's best glasses reach
No fields but are his own.

XXVII

Fish in the unruffled lakes
The swarming colours wear,
Swans in the winter air
A white perfection have,
And the great lion walks
Through his innocent grove;
Lion, fish, and swan
Act, and are gone
Upon Time's toppling wave.

We till shadowed days are done,
We must weep and sing
Duty's conscious wrong,
The Devil in the clock,
The Goodness carefully worn
For atonement or for luck;
We must lose our loves,
On each beast and bird that moves
Turn an envious look.

Sighs for folly said and done
Twist our narrow days;
But I must bless, I must praise
That you, my swan, who have
All gifts that to the swan
Impulsive Nature gave,
The majesty and pride,
Last night should add
Your voluntary love.

XXVIII

Dear, though the night is gone,
The dream still haunts to-day
That brought us to a room,
Cavernous, lofty as
A railway terminus,
And crowded in that gloom
Were beds, and we in one
In a far corner lay.

Our whisper woke no clocks,
We kissed and I was glad
At everything you did,
Indifferent to those
Who sat with hostile eyes
In pairs on every bed,
Arms round each other's necks,
Inert and vaguely sad.

Oh but what worm of guilt
Or what malignant doubt
Am I the victim of;
That you then, unabashed,
Did what I never wished,
Confessed another love;
And I, submissive, felt
Unwanted and went out?

XXIX

Love had him fast, but though he fought for breath
He struggled only to possess Another,
The snare forgotten in the little death;
Till You, the seed, to which he was a mother,
That never heard of Love, through Love was free,
While he within his arms a world was holding,
To take the all-night journey under sea,
Work west and northward, set up building.

Cities and years constricted to your scope,
All sorrow simplified, though almost all
Shall be as subtle when you are as tall:
Yet clearly in that 'almost' all his hope
That hopeful falsehood cannot stem with love
The flood on which all move and wish to move.

XXX

(To Christopher Isherwood)

August for the people and their favourite islands.
Daily the steamers sidle up to meet
The effusive welcome of the pier, and soon
The luxuriant life of the steep stone valleys,
The sallow oval faces of the city
Begot in passion or good-natured habit,
Are caught by waiting coaches, or laid bare
Beside the undiscriminating sea.

Lulled by the light they live their dreams of freedom;
May climb the old road twisting to the moors,
Play leap frog, enter cafés, wear
The tigerish blazer and the dove-like shoe.
The yachts upon the little lake are theirs,
The gulls ask for them, and to them the band
Makes its tremendous statements; they control
The complicated apparatus of amusement.

All types that can intrigue the writer's fancy,
Or sensuality approves, are here.
And I, each meal-time with the families,
The animal brother and his serious sister,
Or after breakfast on the urned steps watching
The defeated and disfigured marching by,
Have thought of you, Christopher, and wished beside me
Your squat spruce body and enormous head.

Nine years ago, upon that southern island
Where the wild Tennyson became a fossil,

Half-boys, we spoke of books and praised
The acid and austere, behind us only
The stuccoed suburb and expensive school.
Scented our turf, the distant baying
Nice decoration to the artist's wish;
Yet fast the deer was flying through the wood.

Our hopes were set still on the spies' career,
Prizing the glasses and the old felt hat,
And all the secrets we discovered were
Extraordinary and false; for this one coughed
And it was gasworks coke, and that one laughed
And it was snow in bedrooms; many wore wigs,
The coastguard signalled messages of love,
The enemy were sighted from the norman tower.

Five summers pass and now we watch
The Baltic from a balcony: the word is love.
Surely one fearless kiss would cure
The million fevers, a stroking brush
The insensitive refuse from the burning core.
Was there a dragon who had closed the works
While the starved city fed it with the Jews?
Then love would tame it with his trainer's look.

Pardon the studied taste that could refuse
The golf-house quick one and the rector's tea;
Pardon the nerves the thrushes could not soothe,
Yet answered promptly the no-subtler lure
To private joking in a panelled room,
The solitary vitality of tramps and madmen;
Believed the whisper in the double bed:
Pardon for these and every flabby fancy.

For now the moulding images of growth
That made our interest and us, are gone.
Louder to-day the wireless roars
Its warnings and its lies, and it's impossible
Among the well-shaped cosily to flit,
Or longer to desire about our lives
The beautiful loneliness of the banks, or find
The stoves and resignations of the frozen plains.

The close-set eyes of mother's boy
Saw nothing to be done; we look again:
See Scandal praying with her sharp knees up,
And Virtue stood at Weeping Cross,
The green thumb to the ledger knuckled down,
And Courage to his leaking ship appointed,
Slim Truth dismissed without a character,
And gaga Falsehood highly recommended.

Greed showing shamelessly her naked money,
And all Love's wondering eloquence debased
To a collector's slang, Smartness in furs,
And Beauty scratching miserably for food,
Honour self-sacrificed for Calculation,
And Reason stoned by Mediocrity,
Freedom by Power shockingly maltreated,
And Justice exiled till Saint Geoffrey's Day.

So in this hour of crisis and dismay,
What better than your strict and adult pen
Can warn us from the colours and the consolations,
The showy arid works, reveal
The squalid shadow of academy and garden,
Make action urgent and its nature clear?

Who give us nearer insight to resist
The expanding fear, the savaging disaster?

This then my birthday wish for you, as now
From the narrow window of my fourth floor room
I smoke into the night, and watch reflections
Stretch in the harbour. In the houses
The little pianos are closed, and a clock strikes.
And all sway forward on the dangerous flood
Of history, that never sleeps or dies,
And, held one moment, burns the hand.

XXXI Epilogue

Certainly our city – with the byres of poverty down to
The river's edge, the cathedral, the engines, the dogs;
    Here is the cosmopolitan cooking
    And the light alloys and the glass.

Built by the conscious-stricken, the weapon-making,
By us. The rumours woo and terrify the crowd,
    Woo us. The betrayers thunder at, blackmail
    Us. But where now are They

Who without reproaches shewed us what our vanity has
  chosen,
Who pursued understanding with patience like a sex, had
  unlearnt
    Our hatred, and towards the really better
    World had turned their face?

There was Nansen in the north, in the hot south Schweitzer,
  and the neat man
To their east who ordered Gorki to be electrified;
    There were Freud and Groddeck at their candid studies
    Of the mind and body of man.

Nor was every author both a comforter and a liar;
Lawrence revealed the sensations hidden by shame,
    The sense of guilt was recorded by Kafka,
    There was Proust on the self-regard.

Who knows? The peaked and violent faces are exalted,
The feverish prejudiced lives do not care, and lost
    Their voice in the flutter of bunting, the glittering
    Brass of the great retreat,

And the malice of death. For the wicked card is dealt, and
The sinister tall-hatted botanist stoops at the spring
    With his insignificant phial, and looses
    The plague on the ignorant town.

Under their shadows the pitiful subalterns are sleeping;
The moon is usual; the necessary lovers touch:
    The river is alone and the trampled flower,
    And through years of absolute cold

The planets rush towards Lyra in the lion's charge. Can
Hate so securely bind? Are They dead here? Yes.
    And the wish to wound has the power. And tomorrow
    Comes. It's a world. It's a way.